I0177921

I Get Happy When It Rains

I believe we are all connected in this life from beginning
to end...

By Tyrone E. Queen

C & C Publishing Company
Washington, DC - USA

Published by C & C Publishing Company
116 T Street NE, #404 • Washington, DC 20002
www.cncpubco.com
© 2017 by C & C Publishing Company
Manuscript © Individual copyright holder

Editor: Carla M. Dean
Cover Design: Shari Bruce
Typeset: Chanelle Flowers

All rights reserved. No part of this book may be reproduced,
stored in a retrieval system, or transmitted in any form,
electronic, mechanical, or by other means without permission
in writing from the author/publisher.
For inquires, contact C & C Publishing Company,
116 T Street NE #404, Washington, DC 20002, USA.

ISBN 13: 978-0-9826531-5-9
Library of Congress Control Number # 2018933975
Printed in the United States of America

This book contains works submitted to the Publisher by the
individual author who verify that the work is their original
endeavor. Based upon the author's affirmation and to the
Publisher's actual knowledge, the listed individual is the
author of their work.

C & C Publishing Company does not guarantee or assume
responsibility for verifying the authorship of each work. The
views expressed within certain poems contained in this
anthology do not necessarily reflect the views of the editors or
staff of C & C Publishing Company.

To T'Mone, Symone and Tyrique,
you have always been my little lights.
So, let your light so shine and change the world...

Acknowledgments

I first would like to thank God for all my life's experiences and all the people I have met along that way. Also, in loving memory of my Grandmother Carrie Hammond for raising me and giving me my religious and spiritual foundation and my Brother Darnell Queen for always being there for me no matter what was going on in my world. I also thank God for my mother Johnnie Mae and father Nathaniel Sr, who were brought together to produce me and allowed me to experience this life on Earth.

I am always indebted to my entire family: step mothers, sisters, brothers, nieces, nephews, aunts, uncles and cousins who all played important parts in all aspects of my upbringing and sense of purpose. Without them, there would be no me.

Thanks to the all the Brothers of Omega Psi Phi Fraternity Incorporated, especially my chapter brothers (Beta Kappa) for helping me to understand and live the principles of Manhood, Scholarship, Perseverance and Uplift! It's always good to be inspired by good brothers and friends.

A few years ago, I worked for a small businessman in Washington, DC and he gave me the task of writing an article in a local newspaper he distributed in the area. It was the first time I had an article that reflected my thoughts written on paper. So, I decided to go further and write my thoughts down and produce this book. Thank you, Mr. Jones and Ms. Ray for giving me an opportunity to share my thoughts.

Also, thank you to C & C Publishing for helping me launch this project and for the editing expertise to help make my words clear and concise.

I can never thank my children, T'Mone, Symone, and Tyrique enough for being my meaning for living and my drive to help make the world a better place for them and future generations. Can't forget all my step-children: Kevin, Kaila, Shante, Brandon and Brittney. Love you guys with my whole being.

With that, I hope your blessings chase you down and tackle you until you acknowledge them!

TABLE OF CONTENTS

PREFACE

Many people feel somber when the forecast calls for rain. Some doctors say people's moods change based on the weather. Feeling compelled to give a distinct perspective on how we see the weather, I decided to write a short book with the focus being on rain. Please keep in mind this is just my interpretation with a spiritual twist, and it means nothing to anyone but me.

I grew up in Washington, DC and was primarily raised by my maternal grandmother, who made sure we had a spiritual/religious background focused on Christianity. We attended a traditional African American Baptist church, and my childhood neighborhood is where I developed my first friendships and relationships. This book reflects my spiritual growth and perspective throughout the years.

My intention for writing this book, which shows the comparison of rain and spirituality, is not to offend anyone's religion or personal doctrine. I would like for people to understand that the change in weather can be viewed from a spiritual standpoint. So, the next time it rains, sit back and look at each drop as a positive event, one that can be seen as part of life's process to the connections we make in our lifetime.

Water is vital to our existence. For example, the human body is made up of 60 percent water. Water is also used in many ways that has nothing to do with our physical being. It's used to take showers, extinguish fires, prepare a meal, or provide the balance and hydration for all living things. If we can imagine ourselves as a droplet of rain that has fallen from heaven, we may realize how we are connected and how we can connect with other people. As we contact others during our life's experiences, we can create a mass or body that can be very powerful and very essential to the existence of life on Earth.

No one is an island. Therefore, you should not live in solitude. Find and share a connection with someone just as each raindrop does when it falls from heaven. On the other end of the spectrum, as sure as the rain will fall, the sun will shine again, and many fallen drops will return to the sky.

So, be blessed in all your activities and look up the next time it rains. Think of the rain as God's way of sending new souls to Earth with the intention of experiencing life to the fullest.

During the rain, each drop tries to connect to other drops. Some drops have a short-lived life on Earth once the sun starts to shine again and the process of evaporation takes effect. The drops will return to the creator sooner rather than later. Let's hope that after each drop has connected and experienced life to the fullest, the experience will allow them to finally settle down in a lake, river, or stream to live out the remaining time left on Earth.

Chapter One

Raindrops from Heaven

A Storm is Coming

I look up and see the sky turn dark as the clouds quickly move in. I start to bubble with excitement because I get happy when it rains. Metaphorically speaking, the rain can be seen as God's chance to replenish the earth. In every drop, there's a soul waiting to arrive on Earth. The problem is you don't know where those souls are going to land. Some drops fall directly into the ocean. Some fall into lakes and streams. Some drops fall on land, which is not always a terrible thing.

When I was young, it would rain, and sometimes these periods of rain would include thunderstorms. If this happened, my grandmother would make us get off the telephone and turn off all electronic devices. Yes, that meant the television, too. When the storm was really intense, she would make us gather in the living room or dining room. I believe my grandmother was just doing the same things that her mother had taught her family when she was a child.

Occasionally, my friends and I would sit on the porch while waiting for the storm to pass so we could go out and continue playing. There were times when we made paper boats and watched as they floated in the water that would flow down the curb and into the storm drain at the end of the block.

During the storms, my friends and I would talk about the rain and why the thunder was so loud. Some would say the thunder was the voice of God and he was angry at us. Sometimes the sun would shine through the clouds while it was still raining and thundering. We would laugh at the older adults saying that when it is raining and thundering while the sun is shining, it meant the devil is beating his wife. As a young kid, I would ask myself if that could be true. I didn't expect my perspective of natural events to change as I got older.

Some raindrops develop into different shapes and forms. Other drops hear and learn different languages and signs. No matter what, like your parents, you are connected to them and they help you to grow. School teaches us to get along with others. However, oftentimes it is not stressed that your interactions with others helps you to gain experience and wisdom.

The drops that fall into the ocean are blessed to be surrounded by many drops. However, the ocean is where many storms develop. On the flip side, raindrops that fall on land have a higher probability of returning back to the creator, sooner rather than later, through the natural process of evaporation.

Your Perfect Place

Raindrops that fall directly into the oceans around the world are immediately connected to other drops that have already been on Earth, traveling through the currents of life. Once those drops connect to the older drops, they form a beautiful body of water. Now, that single raindrop connects to those who can help him. However, keep in mind, there are those who can hurt him, making it stormy.

At birth, we are sent to earth and given parents who connect us to other people, some who may have our best interests at heart and some who do not. You never know who you might end up meeting and where. You may be raised by people of various races, religious backgrounds, and cultures. So, while living your life, you hope the other people

17

you connect with will help you grow and experience the positive side of life.

For example, water is the essence of life and every drop affects humans, creatures, and plants. Some raindrops are collected to make bottled water and become a source of hydration. Some drops make it to hospitals to help heal the sick or cleanse the broken. Others are blessed by a priest and spread on the foreheads of religious followers. Water is also used as a baptismal source to renew a person's spiritual perspective or initiate them into a new religious order or sect.

Water is also used to provide plants with needed hydration. Before a plant grows, water travels deep into the earth and hydrates the seed. From water, seeds receive the strength needed to break through the soil to grow into a beautiful flower, colorful shrub, or a mighty tree.

Water is also collected to fill objects such as pools, which allow people to enjoy them on hot summer days. Not all pools are outdoors, but if they are filled with water, then their source and use are typically the same.

Gained wisdom and knowledge guides us through life and ultimately helps us find our purpose in life. I believe this process helps us maintain our overall mental and physical balance.

No matter where you end up, your perfect place may be a blessing or a curse. It's all in your perspective. It doesn't matter how a person got there and what their experiences were up to that point; they can look back, assess their past, and then chart the course to their best future.

No raindrop should compare themselves to another, because both have the potential to provide an area, community, or society with the highest good.

Chapter Two

Born Unto the World

The Journey with Que

To give you a personal perspective, I would like to allow you a chance to experience the life of a drop, who we will refer to as Que. Que was sent to the earth in 2005 during the storm of Hurricane Katrina. This historic storm devastated the city of New Orleans, Louisiana. In the beginning, Que was overjoyed that he made it to Earth. During his transition, he was tossed around, and it took him a while to find some direction. Mother Earth was in pain in this part of the region, and the reason for the devastation still cannot be explained.

After the storm and flooding, Que went along life making connections to other raindrops that gave him information on how to survive. Just like every new person, Que experienced situations that help groomed him to learn life's lessons and when to avoid trouble.

Years went by, and Que made some friends and deep connections. Que had been around the world and back. He had seen various people and places, along with many different boats and floating devices. As a young drop, he enjoyed the wakes from the passing boats and objects that allowed him to play on the waves and get pushed deeper into the other areas of the ocean.

One day, Que met Sip, an older raindrop who had been on Earth for a while and experienced many different events and situations. She had witnessed the coming and going of many connections and therefore could give Que good advice on how to survive and create new connections with others, as well as provide suggestions on how he could help the other living beings on Earth.

During their conversation, Sip told Que, "One day, you will return to the heaven from where you came. This is just the cycle of life. Getting caught up will happen and returning to the creator is unavoidable."

Confused, Que replied, "Please tell me more. No one told me about the transition of returning to the sky. What does that mean?"

"Que, therefore the choices and relationships you make are very important. You must make connections that will enhance your life and help you experience all the pleasures life has to offer. But, don't be selfish. Always learn to give when the time is right," Sip explained. Over the next year, Sip continued giving wisdom to Que.

"Try to stay away from the solid objects, especially land masses," Sip told Que. "If you avoid solid ground, you can dive deeper into the earth and look for seeds to give the necessary ingredients that will help them reach the surface. You can have a significant impact on others. Just think about what you're good at and the different opportunities available to you."

She also told Que, "We are all born and sent to Earth; however, we all must transition back to the heavens. Just as the rain falls and God appoints you a place on Earth, he will also send the sun, who has the complex job of not only giving and sustaining life but also retrieving life through evaporation. As related to water, the sun is the orchestrator of evaporation."

Que was puzzled after spending time with Sip. No other drop had explained evaporation or mentioned the cycle of life to him. Sip explained what many didn't want to talk about. Evaporation is the process of returning to your creator and finding rest, or getting information for a re-assignment in preparation for another trip to Earth. A reason for one's return to Earth may be so that they can accomplish specific tasks or influence others. Sip also explained to Que that he must make wise choices and not be influenced by the excitement of passing storms.

"Do not get so bored that you find yourself stuck in a rut, because this is one of the worst places you can find yourself," Sip warned. "This isolation can cause pain and anguish to you and others. Your decision not only affects other raindrops, but it affects all the plants, animals, and humans who live on Earth."

Sip provided Que with some valuable information. Information that would last a lifetime. Que thanked Sip for taking the time to explain the unknown. Giving her a wink as the sun glistened off his body, he floated away with the afternoon current, not knowing what life had in store for him or what other connections he would make.

Rough Choices

One day, a collection of raindrops was relaxing off the coast of Southeast Africa, when a high-pressure front developed and swept across the land mass on its way to connect with the unsuspecting drops of water. Behold, a new storm developed. The other raindrops holding on to Que told him that those storms could be very dangerous, that many drops joined because they were bored and in need of excitement. Therefore, they would connect with other drops or souls, creating death and destruction from their strength.

Que thought back to Hurricane Katrina. *This is what was going on when I got to Earth.* It wasn't the best experience to remember, but Que was ready for some excitement!

As the winds increased and the raindrops held on to each other, they made their way across the ocean, seeing and meeting other raindrops who had just gotten to Earth or who had been there for a while. There were many bored raindrops waiting for the next storm, so they could travel to other parts of the earth.

Storms that develop provide raindrops with experiences, which include ups and downs. Many raindrops don't know that the experience of being thrown around can put you in a situation that will land you closer to the end cycle of life. Storms can get close to land, and if raindrops don't hold on tightly, they will be left behind. Storms can also cause destruction to families that live in physical structures. With that said, these storms impact states, cities, and towns.

So, as some storms make landfall, they can affect the inhabitants in the area. This includes people. Many people run for cover and animals seek higher ground. All the while, the raindrops think they are just having fun, not knowing the degree of destruction they can cause together as a powerful force.

I view this situation as a mighty hand slap. This is an example of the power of water and how many raindrops can be a destructive force.

After the raindrops fall upon land and damage has been done, the storm moves on. Some of the raindrops, young and old, release themselves from the collective group and fall to the earth. Some drops are excited about what just occurred. Others are sad at the destruction they caused by being encouraged to join the storm. Many drops decide to move on together as a collective group.

After making it to the Gulf of Mexico, Que lets go of the group. He doesn't want to continue being tossed around, not knowing where he may end up and who he might affect. As he lets go, another raindrop named Drip lets go, too. Drip just arrived to Earth. Que introduced himself, and after a brief conversation, he tried to provide Drip with the same wisdom that Sip provided him with earlier. However, Drip didn't care to hear about cycles of life, land, or even the sun. He only wanted to move on and find the next pleasure in life, not worrying about nothing but himself.

Some choices we make in life are comparable to storms. They impact us for the moment; however, if you can survive, you will gain an understanding from the experience that will add to your wisdom. On the flip side, if you fail to understand your situation, you return to the creative prematurely.

I've experienced these situations and thank God for his grace and mercy. I can testify that I am still here, and by still being here, it allows me the opportunity to explain to younger people that as a raindrop wisdom is gained through the experiences, decisions, and choices we make in life. I hope to translate to the younger people that you must ultimately treat others like you want to be treated.

Chapter Three

Treat Others Like You Want to Be Treated

Thirsty Anyone?

The raindrops that make it through the storms and avoid the land usually find a purpose in life and feel the need to give back. They want to help and encourage other drops as they fall to Earth. Again, these raindrops give life to save or help another life. Many raindrops learn this lesson before becoming transformed and returning to the Creator, who I choose to call God.

As many raindrops navigate their way through life, they learn that there are other places where they can do some good in cooperation with the other inhabitants on Earth. Some drops dive deep into the sea to continue giving life to fish and other creatures that we don't know about or always see.

However, there are water sources that may seem less invasive and destructive. These sources include rivers, lakes, and streams. Many humans who work at stores, carry-outs, and restaurants capture raindrops to be used to prepare cooked fish, steamed shrimp, and other menu items that humans consume.

Then there are the situations we take for granted, the other ways raindrops learn to give back. For instance, the bottled water industry. Raindrops are accumulated in the springs high up on mountaintops and collected by a beverage company, which has manmade devices that help to prepare bottles of water with various labels. These bottles are then distributed around the world to be consumed by people.

Regardless of the situation, many raindrops find their calling or purpose. For example, when disaster or destruction takes place, many relief organizations provide water to those in need. Even though the effect of Hurricane Katrina was devastating, water served a purpose of helping those who had survived.

Water is used to keep the body in harmony. Harmony and internal regulation helps us stay in balance with the earth and God, our creator. Even movement requires our bodies to use water. Ask any runner, football player, or other athlete, and they will tell you how water plays a very important role in helping them to be able to perform. Water is the number one beverage suggested for consumption. For those who live an athletic lifestyle, Gatorade and other sports drinks consist of 90 percent water with electrolytes added.

Streams, Lakes, and Rivers

Streams, lakes, and rivers fascinate me. These bodies of water are usually calm, peaceful, and play an important part in the overall balance of the ecosystem. When considering a drop of rain, if you're blessed to make it to a stream, lake, or river, the opportunity might present itself where you can have an impact in helping the living creatures in that area.

We never know where we will end up. Chances are we may fall in urban areas where there is a lot of traffic, hustle and bustle of life. Connections with other people, or raindrops, may be easy. However, the pace is very fast in these areas, and most times the connections only develop into associations, not deeply-rooted relationships.

As a raindrop, Que found himself in the ocean that resembled an urban area. Some characteristics include unsettled waters with sharks and storms that can develop at any time. Only the drops you hold on to can determine whether you prosper or fail. It should be your goal to stay away from the storms of life and not get caught up in them. Hopefully you'll find your stream, lake, river, and even ocean that fulfills your needs. Some bodies of water are used to make spring or purified water. In other areas, the water is cleaned naturally.

Lakes and rivers are used in various ways. Some ways include using them as recreational areas where people can enjoy fishing, sailing, and swimming. People are not the only ones who take advantage of the calm water, though. Many

37

creatures inhabit these areas to have offspring, build dams, or whatever their instinctive nature allows them to do. Water only plays a small part of the development of life, nature, and happiness.

Some of these bodies of water are carefully designed and sculptured by an intelligent entity who I call God. Again, God is the originator of rain, and the people that populate the earth would not exist if it had not been for the movement of the original mover.

The souls that populate the earth will hopefully develop, make connections with other souls, and experience life to the fullest. While doing so, many souls can contribute to the development of the seen and unseen inhabitants of nature and life.

Remembering this, instead of feeling down or depressed when it rains, I rejoice because I know God is providing Earth with what is needed to sustain life.

Chapter Four

Time to Reflect and Return

Sitting on the Dock of the Bay

As human beings, we experience drama daily. I challenge you to take some time to just sit and reflect. For example, there are docks located just outside downtown San Francisco. From the docks, you can see the famous Alcatraz Prison and the Golden Gate Bridge. But if you take the time to reflect, you will notice the sea lions laid out trying to warm themselves in the sun's rays or the seagulls diving in the water to catch their next meal. Wherever you are, take some time to just sit, reflect, and notice what is around you.

Some people use the sound of water to meditate or relax. During this meditative state, give your mind a break and think of the glory of God.

Have you ever wondered why even with the sun's powerful rays, water never entirely evaporates?

The occurrence of evaporation is constant, and during this process, many drops of rain return to the sky. Each drop has its own history. In a body of water, raindrops hold on to other drops. This is what collectively creates a mass of water. Some raindrops have been traveling for some time, while other drops have just arrived with the morning dew.

A dock, a shore, or a bridge can be used as an observation platform to allow us the chance to sit and reflect, giving us time to take a moment to enjoy the water and nature.

At this point in my life, I see rain and water as a collection of souls holding on to each other and developing relationships. As an observer, we don't know an individual drop of water's date of conception. However, when the forecast calls for rain, this becomes the birthdate of new souls or people who are ready to make a connection. This rain event is a new life that can be groomed and developed over time. This time allows for connections and the development of relationships.

Returning Home

We are all born unto this world, and one day we all must die. I don't mean to be the bearer of shocking news, but this is reality. It's the cycle of life. If you're reading this, you had an ancestor who played an important part in your existence. Without them, you would not be here today. Furthermore, without the initial movement of the Creator, the one who I choose to call God, no life on this Earth would exist.

In my opinion, we all will return to our creator. When comparing death to the rain, every raindrop will one day succumb to evaporation. In that process, they must return home. Even after all of life's experiences, we all must return to the sky or heaven from where we came.

When we compare a rainstorm to the process of life, we see evaporation as a part of life's cycle. The rain falls; people connect with others, build relationships, and experience life. Then the sun shines and its rays invoke evaporation.

The sun's presence is like the biblical Jesus returning to Earth from the heavens and calling his believers home. It's funny how the Book of Revelations references Jesus returning on a heavenly cloud to reclaim his people. Consider how the sun peaks through the clouds each day to make its presence felt and to start the evaporation process. I can say that I truly love the life God has blessed me with and appreciate my life's experiences. We all know life can throw various types of challenges and troubles at us: death of a loved one or friend, financial struggles, loss of employment, strained personal relationships, and other issues. However, I find that when you connect yourself with others and use that experience, it can help you shape a greater perspective in life.

With this new outlook, you'll be better able to realize and relate to Proverbs 18:1, which states, "A man who isolates himself seeks his own desire; he rages against all wise judgment." Hopefully, you'll take the time to reflect on this verse, as it is so relevant to all your life's experiences. Therefore, connecting with other human beings will make you part of a powerful force or better yet a calm, refreshing movement of peace and love.

After reading this book, I hope you will keep in mind that life is a great gift that God has blessed us with and one that we need to take advantage of every moment. We can learn to build on the relationships that can and will develop over our lifetime.

So, the next time you're out walking, running, or going about everyday life, try saying hello to someone. That small greeting just might turn out to be the start of a beautiful relationship. That potential connection may possibly last a lifetime. Remember, ultimately, we will return home to our creator or our source of existence, the one who I choose to call God!

Conclusion

In conclusion, I believe life is all about perception. The next time it rains, I challenge you to see the event in a different perspective. Maybe even try cracking a smile. This may be God's way of cleansing, rejuvenating, and populating the earth.

Connections are important. Therefore, try to make some positive connections and pray that God provides you with the wisdom and discernment to recognize the potential for negative connections so that you may avoid them. Take the time to seek the peace and love that is available if you just look and enhance your perspective.

Make sure you learn something during your connections, even if they include the storms of life. Don't just seek out the next adventure that can have a negative impact on others and cause destruction. Not everyone makes it through a storm and lives to tell about it. I have joined storms, failed, and by God's mercy lived to see another day. God gives us free will to make choices. Be sure you know what you're doing and who will be affected by the choices you make. In other words, please be mindful.

God allowed his grace and mercy on my life to make an impact today in an encouraging way. So, with my new perspective and optimistic influence, I try to relay a positive blueprint to share with those who are coming after me. Building bridges is what I want to do.

To God, I give the honor and praise for all my life's experiences! I have an umbrella if someone would like one, but I will have to share that in another book. May God continue to bless you all. Now go out and build positive connections that can last a lifetime!

List of Contributors

Shari Bruce, Graphic Designer - biggirll@sbcglobal.net

Carla M. Dean, Editor – www.ucanmarkmyword.com

Chanelle J. Flowers, Typesetting - www.cncpubco.net